Unbelievable Pictures and Facts About Boxing

By: Olivia Greenwood

Introduction

Boxing may look like an easy sport but the truth is, you need lots of skill, stamina, and practice to become a boxer. Boxing is a very famous sport and today we are going to learn all about it.

How many types of Boxing are there?

The two main types of boxing that exist consist of amateur boxing and professional boxing.

What needs to happen in order for someone to win in a match?

There are a couple of different ways that you can win in boxing. Usually, the boxer who has obtained the highest score by the end of the game is the winner. A boxer can end any boxing match with a move called a knock-out where they completely knock their opponent out and this makes them the winner immediately.

Do we know the time period that Boxing dates back to?

Boxing really is one of the oldest sports as it dates back all the way to Egypt around 3000 BC. That is so long ago it is even hard to imagine that far back in time.

Were any Greek gods connected to the sport?

The ancient Greek gods certainly did play a part in boxing. There are many myths that boxing was started by the Greek god Apollo. It is said that Apollo actually invented boxing and he defeated any other gods who tried to fight with him. He was the best boxer out of all the Greek gods according to the stories.

Is Boxing a sport that children can do?

Children can start boxing, however, it is suggested that they make use of the correct safety gear and safety measures. It is also important that they take proper classes from professionals so that they don't injure themselves.

What essential equipment is needed for Boxing?

The equipment that you need depends on what level of boxing you are going to be engaging in. Professional boxers need protective headgear, hand wraps, proper boxing shoes, a mouthguard, and other equipment necessary to stay safe.

Who specifically invented gloves for Boxing?

Boxing gloves were actually invented by a man named Jack Broughton, he invented them in 1743.

Is boxing a very dangerous sport or not?

The truth is that boxing can become an extremely dangerous sport. Not only have people died during boxing matches but there are serious risks involved. People have become brain damaged and they have sustained life long injuries.

How are Boxers chosen to fight one another?

Boxers are chosen to fight one another based on various factors such as their weight division, boxing history, and skill level.

What is the best way to learn proper Boxing?

The best way to learn proper boxing is to go to your nearest boxing club or boxing gym. The ideal way to learn is by receiving proper training from a boxing coach who will be able to teach you the proper ways of the sport from the start.

Did any boxer receive millions for an 89-second fight?

Mike Tyson was the boxer who actually received millions for a fight that only lasted 89 seconds. This fight is a very famous boxing fight that most boxing fans will know about.

Have Boxing matches always had a maximum amount of rounds?

The answer is no back in the earth twentieth century, boxing was known to have an unlimited amount of rounds. Over the years this changed and for your interest, a professional boxing match has a maximum of twelve rounds.

On average how long is one round in a match?

Believe it or not, one boxing round only lasts for around three minutes, there is also a one minute rest time allocated between boxing rounds.

Do you have to be in good shape to be a boxer?

You ideally should be in good shape if you want to be a boxer, boxers are actually some of the fittest athletes in the world. You will need to be extremely physically fit to box, as you get tired very easily. It may look quite easy when you are watching the game but when you try it out yourself you will soon see how physically demanding it actually is.

What is an interesting fact about George Foreman?

George Foreman was a world-famous boxer and he came out with the George Foreman grill. This made him more money than he ever made as a boxer and he literally made millions of dollars. These grills were introduced in 1994 and many advertisements were made using George Foreman, it became very popular in a very short space of time.

What Boxer had the nickname "the greatest"?

The legendary boxer named Muhammad Ali gave himself the nickname "the greatest" and he lived up to this nickname many times. His daughter Laila Ali also became a boxer.

Is there a boxer that has had the most knockouts?

The boxer who achieved the most knockouts first in his career was Billy Bird. He achieved one hundred and thirty-eight knockouts during the course of his career.

What is the heaviest weight division in a Boxing match?

In boxing, people are categorized according to their weight. There are tons of different weight divisions but the heaviest one is called heavyweights and they usually are over two hundred pounds or more in terms of weight.

What is the correct way to stand in boxing?

Standing correctly in boxing is extremely important and this is known as your boxing stance. There are a few different boxing stances and techniques but it all depends on if you are right-handed or left-handed. This determines the leg that is in front and your particular boxing stance.

Has professional Boxing been banned in many countries?

Over the years many countries have actually banned boxing for all sorts of reasons. Many countries do not want to risk the damage that boxing can cause. Some countries that have banned boxing include Egypt, Libia, Saudia Arabia, Iraq, Pakistan, and even India.

Printed in Great Britain
by Amazon

73134098R00024